Behind the Scenes

FILM

SARAH MEDINA

Published in 2013 by Wayland
© Wayland 2013

Wayland
338 Euston Road
London NW1 3BH

Wayland Australia
Level 17/ 207 Kent Street
Sydney NSW 2000

Editor: Nicola Edwards
Design manager: Paul Cherrill
Designer: Rita Storey

British Library Cataloguing in Publication Data

Medina, Sarah, 1960-
Film. - (Behind the scenes)
1. Motion pictures - Vocational guidance -
Juvenile literature 2. Motion picture industry - Vocational guidance -
Juvenile literature
I. Title
791.4'0293

ISBN: 978 0 7502 7144 8

The author and publisher would like to thank the following for permission to reproduce the
following photographs and quotations in this book:
© Bob Turner/Alamy p4, © Stuart Kelly/Alamy p5, © Martin Thomas Photography/Alamy p6
© Richard Levine/Alamy p7,© Geraint Lewis/Alamy p8, © Pictorial Press Ltd/Alamy p10,
© brimo/Alamy p11, © *The Guardian* p12, © Keith Morris/Alamy p13, © Shaun Higson
colour/Alamy p24,© Peter Titmuss/Alamy p25, © Steven May/Alamy p27, © Marwood
Jenkins/Alamy p29; Bobby Bank/WireImage/Getty Images p15, Robert Patterson/Getty Images
p16, Indranil Mukherjee/AFP/Getty Images p20, Phil Dent/Redferns p21, Frantzesco
Kangaris/AFP/Getty Images p23; istock pp 1, 2, 9, 12, 14, 18, 19, 22, 26, 28 and 29.
Cover image James Devaney/WireImage/Getty Images

Printed in China

Wayland is a division of Hachette Children's Books,
an Hachette UK company.
www.hachette.co.uk

Contents

Introduction to film

It is impossible to imagine a world without film. Since the first silent films of the early 20th century, film has entertained, informed and educated millions of people around the world. People traditionally watch films in public places, usually at the cinema, or in the privacy of their home, on TV and DVD. Nowadays, films can be downloaded onto computers and mobile media players, too – and even onto some mobile phones.

Different types of film

Feature films last between about 90 and 200 minutes. Many feature films are made to be shown in cinemas; they are then released onto DVD and, later, shown on TV.

Some feature films, however, are direct-to-DVD, which means that they are not intended to be viewed on the big screen. TV films are made especially for viewing on a television. TV and direct-to-DVD films are often made with much smaller budgets than the big cinema releases.

← *Cinema-goers at the Odeon Leicester Square in central London. Film has remained as popular as ever in its longer than 100-year history.*

People see film as an exciting industry – and many want to make a career in it, whether they are in front of the cameras or behind them.

Something for everyone

Film genres are so varied that there are films to appeal to everyone, whatever their age or interests. Action and adventure films are exciting, with big-budget effects and exotic locations. Drama films are normally serious stories, usually with highly developed characters and plots. Horror and science fiction films are tense and often frightening to watch.

Comedy films, from spoofs, such as *Airplane!*, to romantic comedies, such as *Hitch*, all are designed to amuse and make people laugh. Musicals use songs and dance to entertain. Children's and family films are light and entertaining. Animated films, such as the *Shrek* series, use special techniques, such as CGI (computer-generated imagery), to create stories. Actors are used to provide the characters' voices.

About this book

This book gives an overview of the film industry, and the key jobs within it. It includes first hand accounts of people working in film, and it will help you to work out whether a career in film is for you.

Any questions?

Where are films made?

Most people have heard of Hollywood, which is the hub of film-making in the United States. Other important film-making centres are India and China. The British film industry is much smaller, but it is strong and has enjoyed lots of international success over many years.

Working in film

It takes a lot of different people – and many different skills – to make a film. This means that the film industry has a wide range of job opportunities. The key areas in film are development, production, post-production, distribution and exhibition. Film also offers job opportunities in other areas, including transport, catering, accounts and human resources (HR). Within each of these areas, there is plenty of scope for career progression as people gain experience.

Development

Development is the earliest stage of film-making. It is all about planning a film: coming up with and then developing ideas, and obtaining funding so that the project can go ahead. Work in this area includes writing screenplays, preparing budgets and schedules, and getting a film crew together.

Production

Production is all about setting up and shooting the film, scene by scene. There are many different elements involved in film production, from designing and creating sets

↓ *Actors such as Uma Thurman, seen here on a film set in California, USA, know that working in film is hard work and very competitive. It is also fast-moving and highly creative.*

and costumes, to technical operations such as cameras, sound and lighting, to directing the whole process.

effects and graphics are added, as well as different sounds, such as speech, music and sound effects.

Post-production

Post-production is the area that brings everything together into a finished product after filming. During post-production, parts of a film may be cut and other parts pieced together. Visual

Distribution

Distribution is all about bringing a finished film in front of an audience. Some distribution staff are responsible for licensing, which means obtaining the right to show a film to an audience. Others are responsible for marketing the film, so that as many people as possible see it.

THINKING AHEAD

Many people want to work in film, especially as actors or directors, because they want to become rich and famous. However, most people in film are not well-known – and most earn an average income, too. It is much better to work in film simply because you are passionate about film-making.

Exhibition

Exhibition staff are responsible for showing films to an audience. This normally happens in cinemas – from large cinema chains to small independent cinemas. Films may also be shown at national or international film festivals and other events.

Development

In film-making, development is the early ideas stage. Ideas for films may be completely new and original, or they may grow out of material that already exists, such as books, plays and TV programmes. Some of the key jobs in development are script developer and screenwriter.

Script developer

Script developers work at the very initial stages of the film-making process. A script developer is responsible for researching new ideas and finding good screenwriters. When a script developer decides to pursue an idea, he or she works closely with the screenwriter as the screenplay progresses.

Sometimes, a script developer helps to raise finance for a film. In the UK, funding may come from a variety of sources, for example: from organizations that finance British film-making, such as the UK Film Council; from broadcasters, such as the BBC; and from production companies involved with the film.

↓ *Many feature films are based on stage plays. Mamma Mia!, which was a huge box-office hit, was based on a musical of the same name.*

Screenwriter

Without screenwriters, there would be nothing to film! A screenwriter writes the film's screenplay, which contains all the words that the actors say, as well as instructions for the film shoot.

Often, screenwriters write a treatment before completing a screenplay. A treatment is like a brief sales pitch: a summary of the characters, action and style of the film. Screenwriters may send a treatment to a script developer, director or producer, in the hope that they will want to commission the screenplay.

Sometimes, a screenwriter is approached to write a screenplay for an idea that already exists. Some films, for example, are based on novels or biographies. On some films, screenwriters may work in a team. Within the team, different writers are responsible for different parts of the screenplay.

↑ *Screenwriters must be prepared to rewrite a script – often, several times – in line with the film director's vision.*

Production

Jobs in film production are very varied. Some jobs, such as set designer and make-up and hair designer, are very artistic. Some, such as lighting and camera roles, are highly technical. Others, such as producer, are more managerial. This section looks at some of the key jobs in production.

Director

The director is the person who has overall creative responsibility for the way a film is made. It is the director's interpretation of a screenplay that we see when we go to the cinema, or watch a film on DVD or TV.

THINKING AHEAD

To be a director, you need a visual brain, which can picture how a screenplay will work as moving images and sound. Excellent communication skills are important, too, because this is a job that involves working with – and directing – many different people.

↓ *The director Mike Newell oversees the shoot for the film* Mona Lisa Smile. *The cast and crew all have to listen carefully to his instructions.*

During development, directors work with the screenwriter on the development of the screenplay. During production, they work closely with many production staff, discussing ideas and giving instructions so that the film evolves according to their vision. Directors are involved with choosing the cast, crew and filming locations, and with planning the shoot. During post-production, directors work with editors until they are happy with the final version of the film.

Assistant directors

A director's job is a huge one, and assistant directors (known as ADs) are there to help with different aspects of the work. The first AD helps the director to plan the shoot, and then puts together and oversees the filming schedule. The second AD supports the first AD's work. During filming, the second AD manages the call sheet, and makes sure that the main actors are in the right place at the right time. The third AD helps the first and second ADs

in any way that is required; he or she is normally involved with overseeing the extras (who are also known as supporting artists) during a shoot.

Any questions?

What is the best entry-level job in film?

The most junior member of a film crew is the runner. A runner's job is to run errands for the cast and crew – anything from photocopying and typing to driving to making cups of tea! Being a runner can be hard work for little pay, but it is a great way to get a start in the industry.

→ *Some production companies offer work experience placements as runners to people who are interested in working in the film industry. Being a runner can be the first step to getting the job you want.*

Producer

A producer is involved with every area of film-making, from development to distribution. It is often a producer who comes up with an initial idea for a film, and then finds the people to make it happen – including the screenwriter and the director. Whereas a director has overall creative responsibility for a film, a producer has more hands-on, practical responsibility for the business side of the film.

The producer is involved with raising finance for a film. The budget for a film can run into millions of pounds – and, during production, the producer is responsible for the film being made within budget. Films may entertain an audience, but they have to make money, too. To ensure the greatest profit, the producer helps to shape marketing plans and to find distributors for the film.

Any questions ?

Is being a producer more about making money than being creative?

Paul Webster, former head of film at Shine Pictures in London, has produced such box office successes as *Atonement* and *Pride and Prejudice*. He says of being a film producer: "If you set out to get rich you're 99% doomed to failure, you've got to be driven by a passion..."

→ *A producer looks after the financial side of film-making, from raising finance to maximizing profits.*

Production manager

Production managers support the work of the producer. They work closely with the whole team to make sure that the production runs smoothly. For example, they work with unit managers to select locations for filming, and they liaise with first ADs to make sure that the filming schedule is kept to.

A production manager's job can often involve a lot of administration and staff management. For example, production managers may write the contracts for the members of the cast and crew, and are involved with decisions regarding their pay and working conditions.

Location manager

Location managers are responsible for finding locations for a film shoot. They have to make sure that the location is suitable and available, and that it is not too expensive to film there. They agree contracts for using different locations, and they are in charge of the location during the shoot.

➔

Location managers have to consider many things before deciding on a location, including accessibility for cast and crew, and vehicles and equipment.

Casting director

A casting director is responsible for finding actors for a film and for agreeing the terms of their contract. They oversee auditions, and they work closely with the director and producer to select the best actors for the different roles. A casting director needs to have a thorough understanding of acting – and a detailed knowledge of which actors there are to choose from.

Actor

An actor's job involves interpreting a screenplay to bring a character in a film to life. Sometimes, an actor does a lot of research to understand and 'get into' a role. Actors always work closely with the director, so they understand his or her vision for the character and for the film as a whole. An actor normally attends a series of meetings and auditions, before being selected for a job.

Stunt performer

A stunt performer usually takes the place of an actor in scenes that contain potentially dangerous action, or when specific skills, such as martial arts, are required. Stunt performers can be seriously injured or even killed, so everyone takes every possible precaution to reduce risk.

← *An actor studies his script as he waits to be called for an audition. Good casting contributes to a film's success, so it is important that the casting director finds actors who are most suitable for a role.*

↑ *A stunt crew films* Spider Man 3 *on location in New York City, USA. Stunt performers are extremely fit and highly trained people.*

Composer

A composer is a person who writes music. In the film industry, a composer writes original music for a film. The composer liaises with the film's director because, to write the best music, it is important to understand the director's creative vision.

Any questions

Do actors ever do their own stunts?

Yes, some actors prefer to do their own stunts – or, at least, some of them! Daniel Craig, who starred in the James Bond films *Casino Royale* and *Quantum of Solace*, leapt off high buildings and onto moving vehicles during filming. He says, "I've thrown myself into it because I get a kick out of it... It's much better if I stay involved with the filming as much as possible."

Production designer

An production designer oversees the art department on a film production. He or she works with the director to create the overall visual look of the film, which includes the different locations, sets, props, costumes and make-up. As a starting point, the production designer studies the screenplay in detail. He or she also needs to consider the film's budget, so that the design plans are not too expensive. Once designs have been approved, the production designer provides design sketches to the art director.

Art director

An art director is responsible for bringing a production designer's visual ideas into being. Before filming, the art director oversees a team of people who build the set and decorate it with props. During rehearsals, set designers may make adjustments to the set, if necessary.

It's my job!

Tony: Art director

"It's great working with the team and seeing different sets taking shape. It can be quite a stressful job, though. For one, I have to keep a close eye on the budget to make sure that we don't overspend. And keeping to schedule is critical — we'd be in big trouble if the sets weren't ready on time. We usually start work months before filming actually begins."

← The director Peter Jackson is seen here with props from his three Lord of the Rings films. Props are an important part of any film set, and help to make the scene look and feel realistic.

Costume designer

A costume designer is responsible for designing, hiring and adapting costumes for the actors in a film. Depending on the film, they may need to work on period, modern-day or futuristic designs. In order to be accurate, costume designers need to know about the kinds of clothes that people wore at particular times in history. They also need to have a good understanding of each character in the film, so they can get a feel for the clothes the character would wear.

Make-up and hair designer

Make-up and hair designers design and apply make-up for actors before and during a film shoot. They are also responsible for an actor's hairstyle, which may include designing wigs, hair extensions or bald caps. For some films, make-up and hair designers create prosthetics for effects such as scars, cuts and bruises.

← *Actors don't always have to look good! A make-up and hair designer needs to know how to recreate effects such as a black eye accurately.*

Director of photography

A director of photography (or DoP) works to make the director's creative vision for a film a reality. Collaboration with the director and the production designer is essential in this job, especially in the planning stages. The DoP liaises closely with the camera and lighting crews, too, to ensure that camera and lighting choices achieve the desired effect.

It's my job!

Finn: Director of photography

"At the moment, I'm working on big epic adventure film. My job is creative and technical at the same time. I have to translate creative ideas into a visual reality, by making selecting the best camera angles, lighting effects and so on. Before filming, I work out all the equipment we need for the shoot. Then, when filming starts, I oversee the process to make sure that the right effects are being achieved."

Camera operator

A camera operator sets up and works the cameras used for shooting different scenes in a film. Working with the DoP, the camera operator decides on the cameras and other equipment, such as cranes and pulleys, and the best camera positions, for each shoot.

THINKING AHEAD

Camera operators need to have strong technical ability – and a good creative eye so, for example, they can frame a shot in the best possible way. There is a lot happening in a film shoot, and camera operators need to be able to respond quickly to instructions from the director or DoP.

↓ *Lighting is a highly technical area, and DoPs need to understand how to create different lighting effects so they can work effectively with camera operators.*

Gaffer

A gaffer oversees a team of electricians, who set up lighting equipment and power supplies for a film shoot. He or she is also responsible for operating and maintaining the lighting and related equipment during production. Health and safety is an important part of a gaffer's job; he or she needs to make sure that all equipment on a film set meets the required standards.

Production sound mixer

A production sound mixer is the person responsible for recording high-quality dialogue during a film shoot. This can be challenging because the conditions on a film set – for example, on a shoot in a tight space, such as in an underground cave – often make it hard to place equipment such as microphones in the best possible place.

During filming, the production sound mixer monitors the sound quality after each take and, if the sound quality is not up-to-scratch, requests a new take. Then the scene has to be filmed again.

←

A gaffer needs to be able to handle the full range of electrical equipment, from cables to generators, as well as managing the team.

Any questions

Where does the term "gaffer" come from?

One explanation given by people in the film industry is that the name comes from the "gaff poles" that lighting technicians used. The poles had hooks on the ends that could move roof panels to let sunlight in when it was needed to light a set.

Post-production

During post-production, all the hard work of planning and filming comes together. This is where the director finds out whether the final film matches his or her original vision! Some of the key jobs in post-production are editor and re-recording mixer.

Editor

An editor puts together the final film that you and I watch at the cinema or at home. Specialist editing equipment enables the editor to combine camera footage, speech, sound effects, music, graphics and visual effects.

↓ *Film editor Deepa Bhati works on Bollywood films. An editor often works alone, but collaboration with the director is essential.*

During a shoot, much more material is filmed than is actually needed to make a film of the correct length. Every piece of footage that is filmed is stored separately and has its own number. During editing, editors select the very best footage for each scene. Using computer software, they join together the different pieces of footage to form a sequence. All the sequences are then combined, and sound, music and visual effects added in, to make the final film.

Marian: Editor

"I work on a freelance basis, and I have worked on different types of films. Right now, I'm working on a horror film. Although a lot of what I do happens during post-production, I am involved with the film way before then. Before filming, I can give ideas to the director about how to get the best out of the screenplay. During filming, I check each day's shoot to make sure that the story is coming together, and that technical requirements are met. It's a full-on job, combining creativity and technical skills – and I love it!"

➡ *Director Mel Gibson sits at the mixing desk in a recording studio as he and his colleagues listen to the soundtrack of his film* Braveheart.

THINKING AHEAD

Re-recording mixers need to be able to concentrate for long periods. A good ear is vital, because they need to be able to hear subtle sounds and effects. They need technical ability, too, to handle the range of complex equipment required to do their job.

Re-recording mixer

A re-recording mixer brings together the all the recorded dialogue, music and sound effects in a film. He or she may add extra sound effects in the post-production stage, too. Re-recording mixers work in sound-proofed studios or editing suites. They sometimes work with other post-production staff, such as sound editors, to make sure that the level of sound is consistent and that the sound quality is high.

21

Distribution

Without distribution, no one would get to see a finished film! This part of the film industry is, for this reason, just as important as all the others. Films are made to make a profit – and it is through distribution deals that these profits can be made. Some of the key jobs in distribution are distributor, and marketing and publicity manager.

Distributor

A distributor is responsible for obtaining the legal right to show a film to an audience, for example, in the cinema, on DVD or on TV.

↓ Distributors need to weigh up the costs of promoting a film with the profits that can be made from the licensing deal.

This is known as licensing. There are two types of licensing: international, which means that a film can be shown around the world; and local, which means that the distributor can only release the film in one country.

After obtaining the required licence, distributors are then responsible for launching the film, perhaps by means of a film premiere. The idea is to create as much interest in the film as possible, so that as many people as possible pay to watch it, thereby increasing the profit made by the film.

Marketing and publicity manager

A marketing and publicity manager is responsible for putting together a marketing campaign for a film. The purpose of the marketing campaign is to bring the film to the attention of as wide an audience as possible. For major feature films, marketing campaigns can be very expensive, but the idea is that expenditure is rewarded with big audiences, which means big profits.

↓ *A model wears a dress made of shopping bags to welcome guests to the London premiere of the film* Confessions of a Shopaholic *in 2009. Marketing and publicity is all about making a film a 'must-see' film of the moment!*

Other jobs in film

Many of the jobs in film are specialized. However, more general job opportunities are available in the film industry, too. These include jobs in catering, transport, accounts, human resources (usually called HR), and legal departments. Whatever their role, people enjoy having the chance to be part of the film industry.

Catering

Everyone needs to eat – and the cast and crew on film sets are no exception! Film shoots can be very long, and three meals a day – breakfast, lunch and dinner – are often provided by a specialist catering company, which is hired by a production manager. Food is carried and prepared in, and served

← Catering staff work at the hub of film making. Preparing food on location is both challenging and rewarding.

It's my job!

Veronica: Location chef

"I work as part of the catering crew preparing food on big film productions. As a location chef, I come up with menu ideas, which have to be approved by my manager. I then work with the other catering staff to prepare and serve the meals from our massive truck. We work long, hard days and it can be really stressful. Sometimes, I've had to start work at three o'clock in the morning! But I work with a great bunch of people in this mobile kitchen, and I enjoy making sure that everyone is fed and watered. You get to meet some really cool people, too."

from, huge catering vehicles by catering crew. Tea and coffee are also provided throughout the day.

Transport

Transport staff are responsible for making sure that the cast and crew on a film production get to the location of the film shoot. They also transport important equipment, such as cameras and props for a film set.

Transport is more complicated – and essential – than it sounds. If someone or something is missing from a shoot, it can be a very expensive mistake. Films are usually shot in multiple locations, often in different countries. Travel arrangements can be tricky, and permits may need to be obtained. Transport staff need to be highly organized and on the ball.

On big film shoots, a transport coordinator is responsible for overseeing all of the transport requirements. A transport manager oversees the large vehicles needed for production, such as, mobile make-up and costume units. A number of different drivers are also needed.

Any questions

How do I get into film?

Jobs in film are in high demand. Many people who work in film need a university degree to get a foot in the door. However, there are other ways in to the industry. Doing work experience, for example, as a runner (see page 11), gives you experience and contacts that can lead to the job you really want.

↓ *Vast amounts of equipment need to be moved around for different shoots. Without transport staff, filming would come to a standstill.*

Accounts

Accounts staff are responsible for dealing with financial matters, such as paying invoices, for hiring the costumes or props for a shoot, for example; and receiving payments, for instance, from broadcasters from other countries who buy a particular programme. The accounts department is also responsible for staff pay, tax and pensions.

Human Resources

HR is all about human beings – the people who work for a film production company. HR staff are involved with all issues relating to staff employment, from hiring to firing. They can also advise employees who have work-related problems.

Legal

Legal staff are normally qualified lawyers, who can advise film industry staff on a range of issues. For example, they may help HR staff with queries about employment law, or they may advise a director about whether information to be included in a film is libellous. Legal staff may also draw up contracts for people who are involved on a film, many of whom work on a freelance basis.

↓ *Office-based work, such as accounting, HR and legal, is an essential part of the film industry.*

Film and you

Film is an exciting and creative industry. Being part of the film industry can give people a real buzz. Watching a film that you have helped to make – and seeing other people enjoy it – at the cinema, or on DVD or TV, is incredibly satisfying.

The flip side is that jobs in film are notoriously difficult to find – and keep. Even when you are experienced and well-established in film, there is little or no job security. Most people who work in film are freelance. Many films fall through because of lack of funding, and so some people rely on work that does not, in the end, materialize.

On the job, the work can be stressful, too. Working hours in the film industry are long, and people often work under a lot of pressure. Conditions, especially on outdoor shoots, may be uncomfortable. The day-to-day reality of working in film may not match up to its glamorous image.

↓ *It is important to weigh up the pros and cons of an area of work – and film is no exception. Only then can you work out if the film industry will suit you.*

If you are interested in working in film, it helps to find out as much as you can about the industry. Reading this book is a good start! You will be able to find out more information from a careers office or library. The further reading list on page 31 will point you in the direction of some useful books and websites.

Think about the kinds of interests you have, and what you are good at. Do these tie in with a particular job or area in film? For example:

- Are you creative and do you love writing? If so, you could consider becoming a screenwriter.

- Are you into fashion – not just what's in right now, but what people have worn over history? In that case, costume design might be your thing.

- Have you got a good ear for sound and music and are you good with technology? If so, you might enjoy having a job as a re-recording mixer.

THINKING AHEAD

Try your hand at making your own short films. You do not need specialist equipment – a simple video recorder will do the trick. There are lots of websites that will help you to get going; see page 31 for ideas. Even though it is only on a small scale, there is no better way to find out about film than by getting on and making one!

↓ *With a video recorder and a computer with basic sound and editing programs, you can gain some valuable film-making experience.*

↑ *University students on a media studies course get hands-on experience of shooting a film.*

Research the qualities and skills you need to work in the area of film that interests you. For example, to be a film editor, you need to be creative, confident and patient – and you have to be able to concentrate for long periods of time. These are qualities; they are largely to do with your personality. You also need to understand film production and to know how to use specialist film editing equipment. These are skills that can be learned.

If you believe that working in film is for you and that you have what it takes to make a go of it, then research, plan and prepare. It is a competitive world, but it is very rewarding. Do everything you can to achieve your goal. Good luck!

Any questions?

How do I improve my chances of working in film?

Work experience is a fantastic way to gain inside knowledge of the film industry. Most work experience is as a runner. Runners may be at the bottom rung of the film ladder, but they meet all sorts of different people – from directors and producers to production crew and actors. If you work hard and make a good impression, these contacts can make all the difference to getting that important first job in film.

Glossary

audition a short performance given by an actor to show his or her suitability for a part in a film

budget money allocated to a project

call sheet a document that gives the detail of what is happening on each day of a shoot, which is used by cast and crew

cast actors and other performers in a film

CEO chief executive officer – the most important position in a company

CGI computer-generated imagery

commission choose someone to do a piece of work, and tell them what is needed

crane a tall metal structure used for lifting and moving heavy equipment

crew the group of people who work together on making a film

design sketch a sketch prepared by production designers, detailing design issues for film sets, such as mood, atmosphere, lighting colours and textures

edit prepare the final cut of a film by deciding what will be included and removing any mistakes

extra a person in a film – often in the background – who does not have a speaking part. Extras are also known as supporting artists

film premiere when a film is shown for the first time to an audience of invited guests

footage piece of film

freelance being self-employed and working for a company on a project by-project basis

funding money given by a government or organization so that a particular film can be made

graphics visual material used as part of a film

libellous containing false information about a person

licensing when a distributor has the legal right to show a film to audiences, either within one country or internationally

prop an object needed for a film set, such as a doctor's stethoscope or a pirate's sword, to make the set seem natural and realistic

prosthetics appliances made of materials such as rubber, plastic or silicone, which are attached to an actor's face or body to change its shape or appearance

pulley a piece of equipment used for moving heavy objects up or down

schedule a list of activities to be completed on a project, with dates by which each activity needs to be completed

screenplay the text for a film, including the actors' words and instructions for filming

set the collection of scenery to be used for a scene in a programme

shoot when a particular scene for a programme is filmed

sound effect a sound other than speech or music, which is added to a film's soundtrack to make it seem more realistic

take the filming of a scene in a film

treatment a short version of a screenplay, with a summary of the main features, such as characters and plot

work experience a short period of time that someone spends working for a film company, often without pay

Further information

The Creative and Media Industry

The creative and media industry spans a wide range of areas, from film and television to fashion and publishing. It's a highly competitive industry, because the careers it offers are seen as challenging and exciting. People who work in the industry need to combine quick-thinking and imaginative flair with technical skill in their chosen area. They often need to be able to work under pressure and as part of a team.

Film Qualifications and Training

Most people who work in film go to university from school. Many do an arts, or a film or media studies, degree, but this is not essential for all jobs in film. Opportunities are always available for people who show talent and dedication, even if they have not taken a media-specific course.

Books

People at Work: Creative and Media by Jan Champney (Franklin Watts, 2008)

Getting into Films and Television by Robert Angell (How To Books, 2009)

Careers in Media and Film by G Gregory, R Healy and E Mazierksa (Sage Publications, 2008)

A Career Handbook for TV, Radio, Film,

Video and Interactive Media by Walker and Llewellyn (A&C Black, 2004)

Websites

For more information about working in the film industry:
www.skillset.org/film
http://www.skillset.org/film/stories/ (success stories)

This website for young people tells you all about how to make a film:
www.firstlightmovies.com/how_to/

For information about careers in the media industry, including film and documentary film making:
www.prospects.ac.uk/industries_medi a_overview.htm

For information about key job roles in the media industry:
www.prospects.ac.uk/industries_medi a_job_roles.htm

For information about training courses in film:
www.britfilms.com/resources/organis ations/education-and-training

For information about how to get a job in film production:
www.uknetguide.co.uk/Employment/A rticle/How_to_Get_a_Job_in_UK_Film_ Production-100302.html

For general information and advice about careers:
www.connexions-direct.com/ index.cfm?go=Careers

Index

Numbers in **bold** refer to pictures.

Behind the Scenes

MUSIC

JUDITH ANDERSON

Published in 2013 by Wayland
© Wayland 2013

Wayland
338 Euston Road
London NW1 3BH

Wayland Australia
Level 17/ 207 Kent Street
Sydney NSW 2000

Editor: Nicola Edwards
Design manager: Paul Cherrill
Designer: Rita Storey

The right of Judith Anderson to be identified as the author of this work has been asserted by her
in accordance with the Copyright, Designs and Patents Act 1988.

British Library Cataloguing in Publication Data

Anderson, Judith, 1965-
Music. - (Behind the scenes)
1. Music - Vocational guidance - Juvenile literature
2. Music trade - Vocational guidance - Juvenile literature
I. Title
780.2'3

ISBN: 978-0-7502-7145-5

The author and publisher would like to thank the following for permission to reproduce quotations
in this book: p12 BBC Online; p13 *The Independent*; p19 (t) *The Guardian*; p19(b) Monster; p22
The Irish News; p23 TheSite.org; p25 *Observer Music Monthly*.

The author and publisher would like to thank the following for permission to reproduce the
following photographs in this book:
© Everynight Images/Alamy p18, © Joel Wintermantle/Alamy p9, Justin Kase ztwoz/
Alamy p27, © Lebrecht Music and Arts Photo Library/Alamy pp15 and 20, © Trinity
Mirror/Mirrorpix/Alamy pp14 and 25; i-stock cover and pp1, 2, 7, 8, 16, 23, and 24;
Jo Hale/Getty Images pp19 and 26, John Shearer/WireImage/Getty p21, Matt Cardy/Getty
Images p12, Mat Szwajkos/Getty Images p28; Shutterstock p5; Tudor Photography 4, 6, 11,
22 and 30.

Printed in China

Wayland is a division of Hachette Children's Books,
an Hachette UK company.
www.hachette.co.uk

Contents

Why music?

Are you thinking about a job in music? The music industry employs tens of thousands of people in the UK. Some of these people are musicians, singers, songwriters or composers – people who 'make' music. Others are producers and sound engineers, promoters and record label executives, DJs and press officers. The range of careers is huge, yet everyone is united by a single passion – music.

A competitive industry

The music industry is a highly competitive area of work. This is because lots of people want to work in a creative and stimulating environment with music at its heart.

Many people who now earn their living working in the music industry will tell you that they started out by working for free, on a work placement or as a volunteer in order to gain vital experience and demonstrate their commitment to future employers.

↓ *Listening to music, researching it and developing opinions about it are the first steps towards a future career in the industry.*

An unpredictable industry

Many music professionals are self-employed. This means they work on a short-term basis, sometimes hiring out their skills for a single concert or event. This gives them more freedom to decide what they want to do, and when. It also means they don't have the security of a regular job or steady income. Almost all jobs in music involve long hours and a constantly changing routine.

A changing industry

The music industry never stands still. Not only do jobs come and go, but the way music is made, produced, marketed and sold is going through a period of rapid change. This is partly due to new developments in technology. Digital media is transforming the way music reaches its audience. Fifteen years ago, no one had heard of 'downloading' music!

About this book

This book provides an overview of careers in music by looking at the jobs people do. As well as examining skills, experience and qualifications it reveals some of the challenges associated with working in music and answers questions about how to break into this exciting and demanding industry.

⬆ *Working in music can be challenging and unpredictable. You need to be passionate about what you do.*

Any questions

Do you need qualifications to make it in music?

Qualifications depend on what it is you want to do. If you want to teach music, for example, you will almost certainly need a teaching qualification. A business degree might be useful if you want to run a record company. However, qualifications are not essential for many jobs in music. What matters most is that you show talent and commitment, you understand how the industry works and you are prepared to put music first. Excellent communication skills are vital in every job, whether you are playing in an orchestra, managing a band or writing a press release. IT skills are important too.

Making music

Hip hop or chamber music? Pop or opera? Rock or jazz? Music is a wonderfully diverse art form, delivered to us in a wide variety of ways. Whether it's a new album or an advertising jingle, a busker on the street or a West End musical, music is all around us. Composers and musicians are constantly striving to create the very best sounds for us to enjoy.

A working life

Musicians work hard to bring their music to an audience. Performance is only a small part of the daily or weekly routine.

Even though many will have gone through a rigorous musical training, musicians never stop rehearsing, practising and improving. Then there are auditions to attend, agents and bookers to call, sound checks to carry out and promotional tasks such as posting leaflets and updating websites to consider. Travelling can take up a great deal of time, too, especially when on tour.

Fame and fortune?

We all know about the musicians who make it to the 'big time', playing to huge audiences and selling albums in record-breaking quantities. But most composers, songwriters, instrumentalists and singers don't achieve this level of commercial success. Few have permanent jobs, and even members of an opera company or an orchestra are likely to be on a short-term contract that lasts for no more than a year or two.

←

This singer is working with a voice coach to improve her technique in preparation for the next audition.

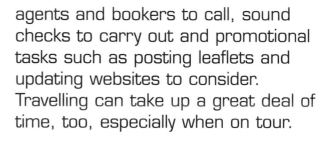

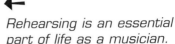

Rehearsing is an essential part of life as a musician.

Often musicians are paid per song or per performance. It can be an unstable way to earn a living and many have additional non-music jobs in order to pay the bills.

Session musicians

Nevertheless, there are all sorts of jobs such as being a session musician, a backing singer or writing music for advertising, computer games, film and TV that allow musicians to spread the risk and earn steadily by working on a range of different projects. Session musicians are hired by the day or even by the hour to accompany solo artists who don't have a band, play an instrument that the band members can't play, record music for advertising jingles or play at promotional events. A good session musician will be able to read music and get it right first time – producers won't pay for you to practise!

THINKING AHEAD

As with all creative jobs, establishing yourself as a singer, a musician, a songwriter or composer requires talent and commitment.

• Get as much experience as you can, performing for free in venues such as schools in order to hone your skills.

• Sing in a choir or join an orchestra or youth band – even if this isn't what you want to do in the long term it will provide you with invaluable training and experience.

• If you want to write songs or compose, get friends to perform your compositions as you'll learn a lot from the way others interpret your work.

• Learn to read music – this is especially important if you want to work as a session musician or in an orchestra.

Teaching and music therapy

Not all musicians and music-makers want to make a career out of public performance. Some people prefer to use their skills to help others learn and experience the pleasure of music-making for themselves.

Teaching music

You love music, and you know a lot about it. Perhaps you play a couple of instruments or sing or compose. Well, teaching music is a wonderful way to combine your passion and talent for music with a satisfying and rewarding career. Remember, however, that teaching requires its own set of skills.

Do you enjoy working with people? Are you patient, flexible, a good listener and communicator? And are you prepared to learn yourself?

Qualifications

Music teachers must be able to read music and play at least one instrument to a very high standard. They usually have formal musical training to degree or conservatoire level. If they want to teach in

schools they will also need a teaching qualification from a college or university. Music teachers who work for private clients don't always have degrees but they will usually have some kind of teaching qualification from a recognised professional organisation.

Music therapy

A music therapist uses music to help clients deal with physical, emotional and mental problems, such as stress, eating disorders, language difficulties or disability.

→

Music teachers help students to develop their musical abilities.

⬆ Music therapists help clients to express themselves and to have fun through music.

A music therapist is not a teacher, and the aim is not to develop musical skill. Rather, he or she† encourages clients to express themselves by trying out instruments, improvising together, establishing trust, building confidence and having fun through sound.

Training and skills

To work as a state-registered music therapist you will generally need to complete a three-year degree course or diploma in music, followed by a postgraduate course in music therapy. This will include work placements in settings such as hospitals and schools. Music therapists often work closely with other professionals such as doctors,

psychologists and speech therapists, and you will be expected to have strong communication skills and work well in a team.

Any questions

What is a peripatetic teacher?

A peripatetic teacher is someone who does not work in one place but travels round from one site to another. Some education authorities employ peripatetic teachers who specialise in a particular instrument, such as the violin, to teach small groups of pupils in a number of schools. Therapists are also used in this way, taking their skills to a variety of clinics, nursing homes and hospices on a regular basis.

Reaching an audience

It is perfectly possible to make music and not share it with anyone. However, most musicians agree on one thing. They want people to hear their music. Reaching this audience is what the music industry is all about.

Doing it live

There's nothing like a live performance. Long before the first download is offered for sale, the first record deal signed, the first world tour announced, musicians have honed their skills in front of an audience of real people who are ready to listen, applaud, dance or, sometimes, walk out.

When musicians are starting out they usually have to organise their own gigs, book their own venues and sell their own tickets. This is all part of the musician's journey. And if you are not a musician yourself then learning how to do these things will give you vital experience if you want to work in the music industry.

Put on an event

The best way to reach an audience is to organise a gig, or, if DJ-ing is your thing, put on a club night. If you aren't a musician yourself, offer your services to a friend's band. You'll need to find and book a venue such as a school hall or

THINKING AHEAD

Promote it!

Find a strong, catchy name for your event. Make posters and leaflets and rope in everyone you can to spread the word.
- Work out a suitable price for tickets (don't forget to include the cost of hiring the venue and any equipment in your calculations) and ask for permission to sell them at your school or youth group.
- If you don't have any expenses such as venue hire then you might want to think about giving out tickets for free. What matters most is that people come!

youth club, decide on a programme, promote the event, make and sell tickets and make sure all the musicians get there on time!

Don't forget to obtain permission from the venue for anything you want to do (such as how late you'd like the gig to finish), and make sure that all the equipment you'll need is in place in advance. There's a lot to think about, but you'll be gaining the kind of experience that future employers in the music business take very seriously.

Get permission

Does your band perform cover versions? Remember that other people's music is protected by copyright. This means that it cannot be performed without permission. Every live music venue must have a Performing Rights Society (PRS) licence and is responsible for providing the PRS with details of any songs performed there.

Any questions

What is the most difficult thing about putting on an event?

Ben Ward, former promoter of local bands and Director of the Tower Arts Centre in Winchester, UK, says: 'Every job has its difficulties. This business is based around getting people through the door and unfortunately that's the only measure of success. You can have a great show, put a lot of work in and really enjoy it but if no one comes to see the act then it's all been for nothing.'

← *If you want to put on a concert or a gig, get your friends involved with ticket sales and publicity.*

Live music promotions

Some people build entire careers out of putting on live concerts and music festivals. Promoters, bookers and event managers all get involved. The job opportunities are varied and exciting but the hours are long, the work is stressful and the competition is intense!

Different jobs

A promoter for a live music venue is someone who finds and books the right bands and musicians for a specific concert or an entire season of events.

He or she will organise contracts and arrange entertainment licences as well as the appropriate marketing and publicity. Other promoters might work on behalf of specific bands and musicians. Their job is to get them booked to perform at

↓ *Michael Eavis (centre) has organised and promoted one of the world's biggest and most famous music festivals at Glastonbury for the last 40 years. He says: 'I liked pop music and people so it seemed like a good idea to put the two together. It was all quite naïve when we started – we really hadn't a clue.'*

a venue, concert or music festival. Promoters also act as talent scouts, looking for new acts and then matching them with suitable events. They may also arrange concerts and live appearances, aiming to showcase the work of new bands or individual performers.

An event manager is responsible for coordinating a specific event such as a concert or festival. He or she will liaise with bookers, acts and promoters to make sure that everything runs smoothly.

It's my job!

Alex Martin of Curious Generation, a music promotions company

"I arrive at the office between 8.30 and 9 am and get through a wad of emails from acts and booking agencies. I'll liaise with our event management team and look at the programme of events that are coming up. The afternoon is usually spent hosting meetings and keeping up with clients. At 8pm I'll head off to watch our gigs or check out new acts."

Any questions?

I want to perform at a live event. How can I get my music noticed by a promoter or a booker?

Musicians and bands often use a 'demo package' to get their music noticed. Sometimes called a press kit, a demo package consists of a CD of your best work (with some smart artwork), a short biography of the individual musicians (names, what they play and/or sing, where they come from and so on), a photograph of the group and any press clippings. Send your demo package to anyone you want to impress!

Necessary skills

Being a live music promoter requires energy, excellent organisation, a sound knowledge of music and business, the ability to recognise talent and great networking skills. Talking to people and building contacts is a vital part of the job.

There are music management courses available that can help you to develop business skills, but many people working in this area will have gained invaluable experience by promoting bands for free.

On the road

← Technicians or 'roadies' set up instruments and other equipment before an outdoor gig.

When musicians tour or travel between venues, they need all kinds of help. An orchestra or band or a solo artist performing in a major arena must rely on 'roadies' – drivers, technicians, engineers, security staff and managers – who travel with them as part of the team.

THINKING AHEAD

You don't need any formal qualifications to be a roadie, but the more skills you have, the more employable you will be.

• Having a driving licence, especially a Large Goods Vehicle licence or Passenger Service Vehicle licence, will give you a definite advantage.

• For some more technical jobs you will need to demonstrate specific skills in electrics, sound production or lighting.

• It is a good idea to have taken a short health and safety course too.

A long day

The roadies are the first up in the morning, unloading and setting up equipment and preparing for sound checks. They also tend to be the last to finish at night as everything has to be packed away after the performance.

Most roadies are paid a day rate. They don't have the security of permanent employment but it can be a great way to participate in live performance and develop a specialist skill such as lighting or rigging.

Specialised work

When bands and artists are first starting out, everyone, including the musicians, tends to share the roadies' tasks. However, success usually means larger, better-known venues and bigger performances. The jobs become more specialised. Some really big acts assign a technician to each type of instrument, for example, to take responsibility for it, tune it and make sure it is in place when the musician needs it.

The sound engineer

Sound engineers operate equipment such as microphones and amplifiers, provide sound effects and balance sound levels. They will conduct sound checks with the musicians before a performance and operate the sound desk during live shows. Previous experience counts more than formal qualifications, and many sound engineers get their first gigs by working for free.

The tour manager

A successful tour manager will be on the road for eight or nine months a year, working three shows and then having a day off. There's a huge amount of preparation to see to, talking to agents and promoters, managing a crew of up to 100 people, booking the tour buses, flights and hotel rooms and coping with last-minute emergencies such as when a musician becomes ill or a flight is suddenly cancelled.

← The sound engineer operates the sound desk during a live gig.

Recorded music

Live performance is one way to reach an audience, but if musicians want to make a lasting impact they need to record their music and find a way to market it and distribute it.

The record company

For decades the recorded music industry has been dominated by companies known as record labels. The record labels have traditionally 'discovered' the artists, produced the recordings and managed the marketing and distribution of the music. Despite the increasing competition from digital media they continue to employ thousands of people to find and develop new talent, arrange contracts and royalty payments, produce the music in the recording studio, organise the artwork and printing for the CD, promote the finished product in the media and arrange for digital content to be made available through a licensed online provider.

 A general admin job can be a good first step towards a career in a record company. As you become more experienced there may be opportunities to apply for jobs in departments such as promotions or A&R (see page 18).

The independent label

Smaller labels known as 'independents' or 'indie' labels are usually set up by people dedicated to producing and promoting a particular style of music. Often these independent labels struggle to make much money, but they are a great way to gain work experience. Being part of a small team means that each person is involved in every aspect of the business.

Digital downloads

Musicians and bands are increasingly beginning to take control of the production and distribution of their music, recording a CD themselves and making it available as a download. But a lot of downloading takes place illegally, without the artist's permission and without any payment to the artist. If you decide to get involved in the distribution of music via digital media, make sure that what you are doing is legal.

THINKING AHEAD

Record companies expect young people applying for a job to show commitment and knowledge about the music industry. Michael Pye, former director of Human Resources at Universal Music UK, has often interviewed people for entry-level jobs. He says that while academic performance is important, experience is what really counts: 'It's a very creative industry and terribly hands-on. Even at the highest levels everyone is involved in the day-to-day business of signing artists and selling music. We like to feel that a new recruit can hit the ground running.'

It's my job!

Jo D'Andrea: owner and director of Jeepster Recordings Ltd.

"Working in an independent record company can be very rewarding because you work on a project from beginning to end rather than working in just one area. You get to work very closely with the artists and you also have greater control over what you do as a label. The difficulties come from not having any financial backing other than your own personal finances – this can sometimes be stressful for everyone."

Artist and Repertoire

Every time a record company invests in a new singer or band, they take a financial risk. Will the artist be worth the investment? The business of discovering new talent, getting a contract signed and then developing a sound that is both original and profitable for the record company is known as A&R, or Artist and Repertoire.

↑ The members of London-based rock band Infadels celebrate signing their record deal with the Wall of Sound record label. Since signing the band has toured the UK and Europe and supported acts such as the Scissor Sisters.

Getting signed

The A&R representative, or rep, is paid by the record company to build contacts in the industry, go to gigs, listen to demo packages (see page 13) and scout out new talent. Once the A&R reps find a musician or band that they like and think will make money for the record company, their job is to guide them through the process of agreeing a contract. This can involve lengthy negotiations over royalties, tour and promotional obligations and the sale of merchandise such as T-shirts.

Finding the right sound

A&R isn't just about getting signed, however. It also involves teaming the artists with the right music, choosing the right producer for the chosen sound, setting a recording budget and even overseeing promotional activities such as interviews with TV and press once the recording is complete.

Building a career

Many people view A&R as one of the most glamorous jobs in the music industry. However, getting paid to do it isn't easy. Many top A&R people have built up the necessary contacts and experience by being in a band themselves, or by DJ-ing or reviewing gigs or promoting bands for free. You'll have to demonstrate a sound insider's knowledge of a particular music scene before a record company will trust you to find and develop new artists.

It's my job!

Alec Boateng, A&R rep for Ministry of Sound

"My role requires me to look for new talent/projects. Then once the artist is signed, preparing the product and introducing it to the marketplace. I have the usual GCSEs, A Levels and a Marketing and Management degree but all the while I was DJing."

Any questions ?

Why do some bands prefer not to sign a contract with a record company?

'Record companies are a kind of army – very regulated,' says Alan McGee, founder of Creation Records and former manager of The Charlatans. 'Whilst live music and merchandise sales are booming, physical [CD] sales are steadily decreasing with more and more fans simply burning tracks from friends or free download sites. The band will get paid more by more people coming to the gigs, buying merchandise and other fees. I believe it is the future business model.'

← *Ollie Cooper of indie band Koopa – the first unsigned band to enter the UK Top 40 through downloads alone. They have since signed a contract with a record company.*

In the studio

The recording studio is where music is recorded and mixed before being transferred to CD or digital media. Some record companies have their own studios, while other studios are available for hire by musicians or record companies. However, it is perfectly possible to set up the necessary equipment in a bedroom or a garage and do it yourself!

Recording and mixing

Each voice or instrument is recorded separately in the studio, so it can be a time-consuming process if the music involves lots of different elements. Then the individual sounds are carefully 'mixed' and balanced to create the finished piece of music, or 'master' track.

It's my job!

Polly Needham, singer

Polly and the Billet Doux recorded their first album in an old brick building because it gave them the particular quality of sound they were looking for. Polly Needham describes their experiences: 'We were keen to experiment with different techniques to find the sound we wanted... We recorded all my vocals late at night because my voice sounds at its best then, with a husky tone I like. Our producer worked alongside the studio engineer and advised him when the sound reached a point he knew we would be happy with. We went back a week later for the mixing process. It is important to leave some time between the recording and mixing so that you hear the music with fresh ears.'

← Sound recording engineer Mike Ross-Trevor at work on a mixing desk at the Sony studios in London. The instruments of the orchestra are recorded separately before they are mixed to create the finished sound.

The music producer

Music producers control the recording sessions, guide the performers and supervise the mixing process. They need to have a clear idea of what kind of sound they want to achieve as well as having technical skills.

Some music producers may work 'in-house' for a studio or a record company, but many work freelance and are brought in by a record company or an artist or band because of their skill in creating a particular type of sound.

Studio engineers

Studio engineers set up and test the recording equipment, monitor sound levels and often assist at the mixing desk. They work alongside the producer, using their knowledge of the technology to create the best sounds and specific effects. The job requires considerable technical knowledge, and some engineers will have taken a music technology course. However others learn on the job, working as an assistant or 'runner' in a recording studio.

← A studio engineer works with Malverde, a hip-hop artist, as he rehearses in a recording studio in Hollywood in the United States.

Any questions ?

I'm interested in producing music for computer games. How can I do this?

Music for computer games, websites, TV commercials and corporate videos requires the skills of a producer who understands how music relates to the image on the screen. One way to develop skills and experience is to record and mix sounds on some home studio equipment, pairing them with video footage or computer animation to see what works and what doesn't. If the images are free from copyright then you can post your finished piece on a video-sharing website and ask for feedback.

Selling the sound

The sale of recorded music is big business in the UK. In 2007, revenue from recorded music was just over £1 billion, making the UK the third biggest market in the world. This means a wide range of job opportunities in retail and digital download companies.

CD sales

Despite the fact that sales of CDs are falling each year, largely due to the increase in music downloads from the internet, music stores and other retailers continue to sell CDs in significant quantities. Getting a job in a music store isn't just a great way to get paid to listen to music all day. It also helps you learn about music trends, gain valuable retail experience and understand how music marketing works.

← *Working in music retail sales is a great way to gain experience and meet customers face-to-face.*

Digital sales

More and more people are buying the music they want through digital downloads. However, despite the rapid growth of digital music sales, careers in this area are still relatively scarce and employees work within a small organisational structure. Entry-level jobs include personal assistants, marketing assistants, web developers and customer services officers.

Employees need to demonstrate a commitment to music, an understanding of digital media and an outgoing, adaptable personality – someone who welcomes rapid developments in the technology.

Merchandise

Selling the sound is about more than the music sales themselves. Increasingly, bands and record companies are looking to sales of associated merchandise such as T-shirts, posters and dvds to promote their brand and increase their profits.

Merchandise is sold at gigs, online and through shops and stores and if you want to gain experience selling your own music merchandise, take a look at websites such as www.overplay.co.uk which offer an online 'shop window' for a fee.

⬆ *It's important to pay for the music you download. Illegal downloads take income away from those working in the music industry, from the artists themselves to the people who clean the recording studios.*

THINKING AHEAD

A degree in marketing proved invaluable for Leanne Sharman, former Vice President and UK General Manager for Napster. She says 'It was a very practical course and I learned about subjects like business law, accountancy and marketing.' However, she says an impressive CV isn't just about qualifications. Proving a commitment to music through experience working at a music venue or managing a friend's band is just as important. 'If I meet someone with the enthusiasm to say "I can see the potential of digital music and I really want to be part of this company," then that's great. I'm looking for that passion when I recruit.'

Music and the media

There are two sides to music and the media. On the one side are those making, marketing and selling music – these people want to promote and play their music through the media. On the other side are those working in radio, television, magazines and newspapers or even writing online blogs – their job is to find out about music and bring it to their listeners, viewers and readers.

↑ *People who work in public relations spend a lot of time on the phone and in meetings, so they need excellent 'people skills' to do their job well.*

Public Relations (PR)

Artists, record companies and retailers all want to get people listening to their music by promoting it through the media. The PR department of a record company, for example, will send out press releases to all relevant media to inform them about a new artist or a new album release. They will organise public appearances and invite journalists to interview their artists, often personally accompanying them from one location to another. They will also try to persuade radio and TV shows to play a particular CD – this is known as 'plugging'.

Daniel Lloyd Jones

Daniel Lloyd Jones now runs his own press company and works for EMI Music Publishing. His first job was as a press assistant at Warners. He says 'In 2004 I was made junior press officer and given My Chemical Romance to look after. No one really knew who they were then; they were just a little Emo outfit from New Jersey. I got them their first Kerrang! cover and they went on to become massive.'

Communication skills

To be successful in PR you'll need to have great communication skills in order to build and maintain contacts in the media. You'll also need to be diplomatic, meeting the requirements of your employer while recognising the pressures faced by journalists, DJs and editors. A good telephone manner and excellent writing skills are essential. An ability to spot new media opportunities will help, too!

Work placements

Some record companies offer work placement schemes in their PR departments. Usually this involves answering phones, photocopying press releases and acting as an assistant, or runner in the office. The work will almost certainly be unpaid, but it is a fantastic way to find out about PR and the music media.

THINKING AHEAD

Sarah Hand, resourcing officer at Universal Music UK says: 'We look for experience such as work placements at a record label or doing music writing for the student newspaper. Something that shows someone is passionate about music, that it's part of their life and that they have some understanding of how the industry works.'

← The members of Take That face journalists, photographers and TV crews at a press conference in November 2005 as they announce that the band is reforming. Organising press conferences is an important apect of a job in PR.

Working in radio

One of the best things about radio is the enormous variety of shows and stations dedicated to particular kinds of music. Whether your interests are classical, country, world music or indie, a job in radio enables you to work in a fast-moving environment, surrounded by the music you love!

The producer

Radio producers work for a specific programme or show. Their role is to manage the show from behind the scenes, helping to select the music, talking to 'pluggers' from record companies, controlling the running order, booking interviews with guests and supporting (and sometimes training) the presenter. It isn't all about the live broadcast, though. There's paperwork to do, and the day usually starts and ends in the office.

The presenter

The presenter or DJ hosts the show, introducing the music on air, talking to guests and often controlling the cues for clips, jingles and pre-recorded interviews.

▲ *Recording artist Lemar congratulates DJ Jon Scragg at the launch of radio station Smooth FM. Different radio stations cater for a range of musical tastes.*

The job demands excellent communication skills, a clear speaking voice, the ability to remain calm and cheerful under intense pressure as well as a passion for music that the audience can connect with.

A national radio show will have a big team of producers, broadcast assistants and editors to support the presenter and prepare sequences in advance, but smaller stations require the presenter to do several jobs at the same time – often acting as producer and editor as well as DJ.

The runner

Runners are general assistants whose job can involve anything from sorting the post, fetching coffee, logging music as it comes into the office, ordering stationery, issuing passes to guests and staff and helping to sort out problems as they occur. It's a great entry – level job as you'll get to see how radio works as well as meet guests and listen to new music before anyone else does.

Some radio stations offer work experience but competition is huge so you'll need to demonstrate your knowledge and commitment as well as good organisational skills if you want that place.

↓ *Working in radio sometimes involves helping out at outside broadcasts or 'roadshows' as well as being based in a studio.*

Any questions

Do you have to be really pushy to get a job in radio?

No one wants the hassle of working with someone who doesn't know when to back off or keep quiet. However, you do need to be confident and determined if you want to get noticed. You'll have to call people who don't know you and persuade them to take you on but most employers don't mind this just as long as you are polite. Being polite doesn't mean you can't be persistent – remember that employers are looking for people who are good communicators, work hard and can operate as part of a team.

Music journalism

If you love music and you love writing about it, music journalism may be the career for you. There are lots of ways you can do this: work for a magazine or newspaper, create a fanzine, write reviews or start your own online music blog.

News, reviews and interviews

Newspaper and magazine editors expect the journalists they hire to be experienced writers. So how does an aspiring music journalist get experience?

The answer is, by going to gigs and concerts, interviewing artists and writing reviews they can post online or send out to some of the smaller publications or a particular type of music.

Try reviewing your friends' music, or an album that has just been released. Be honest and aim to give your writing a distinctive voice or tone. Develop a critical approach by reading the work of other music journalists. Look online and in newspapers and magazines.

← A reporter from Rolling Stone *music magazine in the United States interviews band members from Taking Back Sunday, My Chemical Romance and Linkin Park as they announce a tour in 2007. Filming an interview is a good way of keeping a record of what has been said.*

28

Building a career

Most music journalists work freelance, so building a reputation for a certain writing style or coverage of a particular kind of music will help your writing to stand out from the crowd.

If you want to get a permanent job with a magazine or fanzine make sure you've got good typing and computer skills and be prepared to work as the office junior for a while. This will help you gain the experience to take on jobs such as editorial assistant, with some writing responsibilities. Once you have been published, keep all your clippings – they will be your passport to more work.

Get blogging

A blog is another name for an online diary or web journal. For many, blogging is a form of instant publication. There is no faster way to reach your potential audience. Whether you want to hone your writing skills and get noticed as a music journalist, or simply want to take part in an ongoing conversation about the kind of music you love, the blog is increasingly becoming the medium of choice for many people across the music business.

Any questions

I want to write for a major music magazine. What qualifications will I need?

Some editors will expect you to have an NCTJ qualification from the National Council for the Training of Journalists. However, a sample of your writing as well as some original ideas for features is more likely to get you noticed. It is important to remember that editors need writers who can deliver their work on time, with the right amount of words, in a style appropriate for their publication.

THINKING AHEAD

Tips for blogging:
- Register on www.blogger.com or a similar blog host (tell a responsible adult what you are doing).
- Give your blog a catchy name and a clear focus. What kind of music are you writing about, and why?
- Aim for a distinctive voice or tone – try writing as if you are talking to someone.
- Update regularly – daily is good.
- Avoid bad language, don't copy someone else's work and don't say anything you might regret later.
- Tell all your family and friends to read it and spread the word!

Glossary

A&R or 'Artist and Repertoire' people employed by a record company to discover and develop new artists and match them with the right music

blogging publishing your views, opinions and reviews online

booker sometimes known as a booking agent; arranges for an artist or band to appear at a live concert or gig

chamber music a form of classical music written for a small number of instruments

conservatoire a school or college for the study and performance of classical music

copyright a form of legal protection for artists that prevents anyone from copying or using their work without their permission

degree a university-level qualification

demo package a tool for getting your music noticed; consists of a CD of your music, photos of you, any press cuttings and a few biographical details

digital media a way of delivering material such as music through digital tools such as the internet (music downloads, for example)

diploma a type of qualification

distribute to make available; for example getting CDs into the shops

fanzine a magazine for fans of a particular artist or band

marketed getting a product noticed and sold

mixing merging sounds recorded separately to produce a finished recording

music therapist someone who uses music to help clients deal with a range of problems

networking building contacts through meeting people

plugging trying to get a particular music track played on radio or TV

postgraduate a higher degree taken after a first university degree

press officer someone who deals with the media on behalf of an artist or a company

press release a statement issued to the media, giving information about a new product or artist

producer the person who controls the recording process in the studio

promoter someone who matches artists with the right gigs and events

PRS licence permission from the Performing Rights Society to perform someone else's work

record label the record company; large record companies may have different labels for different types of music

roadie a person who travels with an artist or band while they are on tour; technical crew, drivers and security staff are all 'roadies'

royalty an artist's earnings from CD sales or from the use of their music by advertisers, film makers and so on

runner an assistant working for a radio station

running order the sequence or order in which different music tracks are played

scout a talent spotter

self-employed working for yourself

sound check a test carried out before a gig or a recording to make sure that all the equipment is working properly

sound desk the technical controls operated by a sound engineer

sound engineer a technician who helps the musicians achieve the best sounds

tour manager the person who makes all the arrangements for a tour and sorts out any problems during the tour

web developer someone who designs new website applications

work placement a short period of work experience, often unpaid, with a specific company

Further information

The Creative and Media Industry

The creative and media industry spans a wide range of areas, from film and television to fashion and publishing. It's a highly competitive industry, because the careers it offers are seen as challenging and exciting. People who work in the industry need to combine quick-thinking and imaginative flair with technical skill in their chosen area. They often need to be able to work under pressure and as part of a team.

Book

People at Work: Creative and Media by Jan Champney (Franklin Watts, 2008)

Websites

www.bbc.co.uk/music/introducing/advice/
This BBC website contains lots of detailed job profiles along with practical advice on applying for work experience placements.

www.makeitinmusic.com/
The 'ultimate guide to help you succeed in the music business', with interviews and advice.

www.young-enterprise.org.uk/programmes/secondary_and_further_education/quickstart_music
If you are aged between 13 and 16 this site will explain how you can set up and run your own music enterprise scheme at school, putting on a music event or producing and selling a music product.

www.overplay.co.uk
This is a commercial site designed to give unsigned artists a platform to be seen and heard and sell their music online. Great for seeing how other people do it!

www.careersinmusic.co.uk
This site is full of relevant, practical information and advice for anyone seeking a career in the music business. It gives useful addresses, job profiles and valuable 'workshops' on setting up a home studio, recording and mixing sounds and so on.

www.www.bbc.co.uk/1xtra/events/get_aheadaz.shtml
This site offers a list of music-related careers from A&R to video director. Jobs are presented with links to professionals discussing their role in the industry and there are links to potential employers too.

www.nhscareers.nhs.uk/details/Default.aspx?Id=432
Clear information about the principles of music therapy and the variety of work carried out by music therapists.

Index

Numbers in **bold** refer to pictures.